Mysterious Encounters

VAMPIRES

by Bonnie McMeans

KIDHAVEN PRESS
An imprint of Thomson Gale, a part of The Thomson Corporation

THOMSON

™

GALE

Detroit • New York • San Francisco • San Diego • New Haven, Conn. • Waterville, Maine • London • Munich

Picture Credits:
Cover, © CORBIS/SYGMA
Akg-images, 7
Bridgeman Art Library, 20
© Bettmann/CORBIS, 25, 29
© Ed Bock/CORBIS, 12
© Bill Diodato/Photex/ZEFA/CORBIS, 8
© Michael and Patricia Fogden/CORBIS, 21
© CORBIS/SYGMA, 26
Amicus/RF/The Kobal Collection, 11
Goldwyn/Film Foundry/The Kobal Collection, 39
Hammer/The Kobal Collection, 16
Toho/The Kobal Collection, 14, 19
The Kobal Collection, 14, 19
Bishop Sean Manchester, 35 (both)
Mary Evans Picture Library, 30

LIBRARY OF CONGRESS CATALOGING-IN-PUBLICATION DATA

McMeans, Bonnie, 1955–
Vampires / by Bonnie McMeans.
p. cm.—(Mysterious encounters)
Includes bibliographical references and index.
ISBN 0-7377-3476-0 (hard cover : alk. paper) 1. Vampires—Juvenile literature.
I. Title. II. Series.
BF1556.M36 2006
398'.45—dc22

2005034832

Printed in China

Contents

Chapter 1

BLOODSUCKERS OF THE NIGHT

In 1923, a woodcutter who lived in Washington, D.C., was on his way home from work one evening. As he passed by a cemetery, he saw a woman in white float through the sealed door of a burial vault into the night air. The frightened man told several people what he had seen. No one believed him, though, until he turned up dead with teeth marks on his neck. Someone or something had drained the man's body of all his blood.

Guards began to watch over the tomb. Then one evening they, too, saw a mysterious woman leave the vault and head toward the woods nearby. Local citizens feared the spirit belonged to a young woman who had been found dead with two puncture wounds on her neck many years before. Like the woodcutter, her body was drained of blood.

The citizens decided to take action. They opened the vault and found that a large, flat stone had been moved away from the top of a coffin. When they lifted the coffin lid, they saw a young woman with fangs like a wolf's, her lips coated in blood. To the terrified citizens, their discovery meant only one thing: They had found a vampire.

In this scene from a 1971 horror movie, a female vampire rises from her coffin after a man removes the lid.

Night Stalkers

Vampires are creatures that are believed to sleep in a grave or coffin by day and walk the earth at night. Their favorite is human blood. They use two sharp teeth to pierce the neck of a victim, then they drink the person's blood.

People around the world have told vampire stories for centuries. In fact, several countries have their own versions of evil spirits who live off the blood of others. For example, in Russia, vampires are believed to have teeth made of steel. In Bulgaria, vampires have only one nostril. In Poland, a vampire's tongue is pointed or sharp like the end of a fishhook.

Most vampire stories are regarded as **legends**. The legends began hundreds of years ago because many people were uneducated and **superstitious**. Vampire stories were especially common in small towns and villages in Europe, where anything out of the ordinary was viewed with suspicion. For instance, villagers feared that a baby born with teeth or with a

Blood on the Lips

As a body decays, blood may escape from the lungs and dry around the mouth. This fact explains why some corpses looked like they had been feasting on blood.

Two vampire bats swoop down to feed on a sleeping wolf in this old illustration.

strange birthmark might grow up to be a vampire. If someone suffered a violent death or a cat jumped over his or her grave, villagers thought that person might become a vampire. Because people knew very little about the causes of disease and infection, they sometimes blamed a vampire if several people suddenly became sick or died around the same time.

There were many common beliefs about vampires. For one thing, vampires usually looked like everyone else, especially when they kept their fangs hidden. A vampire could be standing among a group of people, and they would never know it. People also believed vampires could change into many different kinds of animals, such as wolves, owls, cats, and bats. They could even change into a mist so they were able to go under doors or through a crack in a window.

People once believed that hanging garlic near windows and doors protected the home from vampires.

Another widespread belief was that vampires **hypnotized** their victims before an attack so they would not fight back or remember anything afterward. Victims often felt weak and depressed the day after a vampire attack. Sometimes, they became infected with a fatal disease. They might have nightmares before they died.

When people suspected that a vampire walked among them, they tried to protect themselves. Some kept a silver cross, blessed by a priest, nearby.

Others hung garlic on their front doors or painted crosses on them. Still others decided to build their homes near water because they believed vampires hated water.

If individuals suspected a vampire had bitten them, they sometimes tried to locate the vampire's grave so they could eat some dirt from it. They believed this kept them from becoming vampires themselves. In order to eat the dirt, however, the victims had to find the grave first.

In Search of the Vampire

To find a vampire's grave, villagers sometimes visited the cemetery and searched for finger-sized holes in the dirt. Because vampires could change into a mist, villagers believed vampires could escape a grave through such holes. Other times a black horse was brought to the cemetery. If the horse walked around a certain grave instead of across it, villagers were convinced that grave belonged to a vampire.

Why Garlic?

Garlic was believed to keep disease-carrying insects, like bloodsucking mosquitoes, away. It is possible people thought garlic would work just as well with vampires.

When villagers thought a grave contained a vampire, they dug it up. If the body looked like it had not started to **decompose**, they became alarmed. They did not understand that a corpse sometimes has a reddish complexion for a while. It might look full or bloated, as if it has recently eaten. It might even make a groaning sound if it is disturbed. Without knowledge of the decomposing process, frightened villagers interpreted all these signs to mean one thing: vampire!

Destroying the Vampire

Once people found a vampire's grave, they usually decided to trap or destroy the creature before it could strike again. To catch a vampire, villagers sometimes left a small bottle of food nearby. If the bottle filled with mist, they knew the vampire had gone in to get the food, so they quickly capped the bottle and threw it into a fire.

There were more gruesome methods for destroying a vampire too, especially if villagers suspected it had attacked someone. After digging up the corpse, they might nail its skull to the coffin, cut off the head, or remove and burn the heart. For further protection, some mixed the ashes with water and drank it. The most popular methods for killing a vampire were to drive a wooden stake through its heart or to shoot it in the heart with a silver bullet that had been blessed by a priest.

Of course, the easiest way to prevent vampire attacks was to make sure a potential vampire would be unable to leave the grave in the first place. A family who thought their loved one could become a vampire after death might bury the person facedown so he or she would dig the wrong way to be free. Another tactic was to bury the body with the stems of a wild rosebush, so the thorns would keep the person from moving about. An iron rod was sometimes driven into the coffin to accomplish the same thing. Still other methods were to tie the body up or pile stones on top of the grave to keep the vampire from escaping.

Actor Donald Sutherland prepares to drive a wooden stake through the heart of a sleeping vampire in a still shot from a 1960s vampire movie.

Plastic white fangs, a long black cape, and penciled-in scraggly eyebrows turn a young boy into a convincing vampire for Halloween.

"I Vant to Drink Your Blood!"

Today, most people do not worry about vampire encounters. In fact, children and adults alike think it is fun to dress up as vampires for Halloween. They visit costume stores to try on vampire capes. They hold up two white plastic fangs against their own teeth and say, "I vant to drink your blood!" There are some, however, who believe that vampires really exist. And to them, vampires are no joking matter.

Chapter 2

VAMPIRE SIGHTINGS AND ATTACKS

V ampire sightings and attacks have been reported many times throughout history. Often the vampires were thought to be deceased relatives, neighbors, or friends who came back from the grave to harm the living. Sometimes the relative was even a child, as in the case of Sarah Tillinghast.

The Vampire Daughter

Sarah was the oldest daughter of fourteen children born to Stuckley Tillinghast and his wife, Honor. The Tillinghasts ran a successful business selling apples and pears in Rhode Island in the late 1700s.

One night Stuckley Tillinghast had a disturbing dream, which then came back night after night. In the dream, he heard Sarah calling to him in the family orchard. When he turned to look for her, she was gone. When he went back to work, he saw a horrifying sight. "All the leaves had turned brown, and the fruit was rotting on the branches," Stuckley said. "A smell of decay washed over me, and I was nearly ill. Stepping back, I saw that fully half the orchard was dead!"[1]

Stuckley worried his dream was a bad **omen**. His fears were confirmed when Sarah became ill and

This still shot from a horror movie shows a terrifying vampire baby.

Shrinking Skin

The skin around hair and nails begins to shrink as a body decomposes. This condition might explain why a corpse's hair and nails seem to grow after death.

died a few months later, in the winter of 1796. Over the next two years, five more children died, just like the fruit trees in Stuckley's dream.

According to one historian, the children all complained before their deaths that their sister Sarah came "every night and sat upon some portion of the body, causing great pain and misery."[2] Then Stuckley's wife became sick. Soon she, too, reported that Sarah was visiting her bedside.

Stuckley worried that Sarah was a vampire. He gathered his neighbors, and they went to the family graveyard to dig up the bodies of all six children. When they did, they saw a disturbing sight. Five of the children had begun to decompose, but Sarah's eyes were open, her hair and nails had grown, and her veins appeared to be filled with fresh blood. Stuckley cut out Sarah's heart and burned it on a rock. Afterward, Honor Tillinghast soon recovered.

A vampire wife prepares to feed on her unsuspecting husband's neck in a scene from a 1970s horror movie.

The Vampire Wife

Vampire relatives did not always attack family members related by blood. Sometimes vampires attacked their own spouses. One such attack occurred more than a hundred years ago, when a man named Jack married and settled with his bride in a country house in Devonshire, England. One day, Jack's friend came to visit for a few days. When the friend arrived, he was astonished to see that

Jack was in very poor health. He was listless and seemed to be wasting away.

Jack's wife, by contrast, was gorgeous. Her flawless skin was pure white, and she had long fingernails painted bright red. Although the wife appeared healthy, Jack noticed she barely touched her dinner when the three dined together.

After dinner, Jack's friend suddenly felt tired and went to bed. The next morning, he awoke to find a mysterious red mark on his neck. The second night, he dreamed of a woman who entered his room and put her lips on his neck in the same spot where he had found the red mark the day before. The next morning, the mark on his neck was infected.

The last night of his stay, Jack's friend was determined to stay awake. At midnight, he watched in horror as Jack's wife came into the room and approached his bed. He waited until he could almost feel her lips on his neck, and then he grabbed her. But she wiggled free and fled the room. The friend left the next morning, certain that Jack's wife was a vampire. A short time later, he heard that his friend Jack had died.

The Vampire Neighbor

Another vampire attack in England involved a vampire neighbor. Dr. Augustus Hare tells the story in his autobiography, *Memorials of a Quiet Life*, published in 1871. Hare's story begins with a young woman and her two older brothers deciding to rent a country house in Cumberland County. One warm summer night, the woman went to bed early in her bedroom on the first floor. She kept her shutters open to admire the beautiful night sky.

Suddenly, she saw two flickering lights that seemed to be coming toward the house from across a nearby field. As the lights grew closer, she could see they were not lights at all, but the eyes of a hideous creature with brown, wrinkled skin. It was heading straight for her bedroom window.

The young woman tried to scream, but she was too terrified. Helplessly, she watched the monster use a long, bony finger to peck at her windowpane until it fell to the floor. Then the creature reached inside and opened the window latch. Hare explains, "[The creature] came up to the bed, and it twisted its long bony fingers into her hair, and it dragged her head over the side of the bed, and it bit her violently in the throat."[3]

At this point the young woman was able to scream, which woke her brothers. But they could not rescue her because her bedroom door was locked from the inside. When they were finally able to break down the door, the creature was gone, and their sister lay unconscious on her bed. Blood flowed from two puncture wounds in her neck.

The young woman recovered, but over the next several months, her brothers slept in a nearby bedroom and kept their pistols loaded. The sister kept her bedroom door unlocked at all times. The following spring, she awoke one evening to

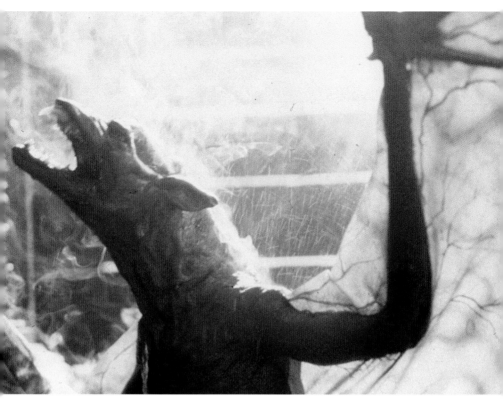

A vampire in the form of a bat is destroyed as sunlight comes streaming in through a bedroom window.

hear a scratching sound on her windowpane. On the window ledge, the same brown creature stared at her with its glowing eyes. This time, the sister screamed as loud as she could. Her brothers heard the screams and grabbed their pistols. They chased the creature across the field toward a cluster of trees. One of the brothers thought he shot the creature in the leg as it ran.

The brothers followed the creature to the nearby burial vault of a family that had died off long ago. Then it disappeared. The next morning,

This illustration shows a group of men in a graveyard firing on a vampire asleep in his coffin.

the brothers explored the vault and found several open coffins with parts of mangled corpses lying about. Only one coffin was intact. They lifted the lid and saw the ghastly creature that had attacked their sister. One of the creature's legs had a bullet in it. Quickly, the brothers removed the corpse and burned it. Their sister was safe once more.

The Voodoo Vampire

Vampire attacks did not occur only in the country. In 1905, James H. Connelly wrote a magazine article about a vampire attack in New York City. In his article, Connelly described a musician named Alonzo, who performed in nightclubs. One night Alonzo saw a man named John Alden who he believed had stolen his girlfriend many years before. Alonzo wanted revenge, so he visited Mama Mokele, a woman who specialized in voodoo. She took some blood from Alonzo's finger and mixed it with other potions to create a spirit bat that would kill for fresh blood. She called this bat "the bat of death."[4]

Mama Mokele placed the bat in a small box and told Alonzo to slip the box into Alden's coat pocket. Alonzo followed her instructions. Alden found the box, opened it, and saw what looked like a small red stain. He thought nothing of it and

Although vampire bats do drink the blood of other mammals, they do not feed on humans.

went to bed. That night he suffered nightmares and dreamed he was drowning. When he woke up, he was bleeding from the neck and felt too weak to get out of bed.

The next night, Alden awoke to see a bat flying away from his hand. When he looked down, both of his hands were badly cut and bleeding. On the third night, he asked a doctor and a servant to keep watch over him while he slept. Soon they saw the bat, too.

The two men cornered the bat on the floor and stomped it to death. When the bat died, "it burst 'like a huge capsule of blood,'"[5] wrote Connelly. The following day, Alonzo was found dead in his room. A doctor said he died of a broken blood vessel.

Alden was not the first person to consult a doctor for aid with a possible vampire problem. Throughout history people asked respected members of their communities for help after a vampire sighting or attack.

Chapter 3

VAMPIRE SLAYERS

Vampire slayers were often soldiers, priests, and doctors. Other times, they were the strongest and bravest men in town.

The Captain and the Vampires

One soldier who helped **exorcise** vampires was Count de Cabreras, an army captain in Hungary in 1715. One day de Cabreras heard a report that a peasant had died mysteriously during the night. Witnesses said the peasant's father had paid him a visit the day before—but the father had been dead for ten years.

The captain interviewed everyone who had seen the ghost, then ordered the father's body to be **exhumed**. To everyone's surprise, "his blood was like that of a living man,"[6] according to a report.

The captain ordered the body's head to be cut off and the body to be buried again.

Soon more peasants came to de Cabreras for help. A family claimed a relative who had been dead for more than 30 years had visited their home three times. The first time he returned, he bit the neck of his brother and drank his blood. The second time, he bit the neck of his son. The third time, he attacked a servant. All three victims died immediately.

De Cabreras told the family to open the man's grave and examine his body for anything out of the ordinary. The family reported that blood seemed to flow through the body's veins. Immediately, the captain told the family to drive a large nail into the body's forehead. After that, they buried the body again, and the attacks stopped.

The Archbishop and the Vampire

Soldiers were not the only professionals that people went to for help getting rid of vampires. Because vampires were considered evil, villagers consulted their local priests as well. One such priest was the archbishop at a church in a Russian province in the early 1800s. A powerful and cruel governor ruled the province. He was so cruel he forced a pretty young woman to marry him even though she loved another. Then he beat her and kept her locked in her room. He also forbade her to remarry if he died. If she did, he said, he would come back to life and kill her.

Groaning Corpses

If a stake is hammered into a corpse, air trapped inside the lungs escapes, causing a groaning sound. Vampire slayers mistakenly thought the groans were proof the corpse was alive.

A fanged vampire lets out a groan after a wooden stake is driven into his heart.

A little while later, the governor did indeed die, and his widow became engaged to the young man she had always loved. After their engagement party, the woman went to bed. Soon she began to scream. When her servants ran into her room, they found she had fainted. She was badly bruised and bleeding from a puncture wound in her neck.

A guard who was stationed at a nearby bridge said he had seen a mysterious black carriage rush across the bridge toward the woman's home. It was coming from the direction of the cemetery where the governor was buried. Night after night,

A vampire hunter holds up a cross for protection from attack in a movie scene.

the carriage returned. Each time, the widow would wake the next morning, bruised and bleeding from the neck.

In desperation, the widow went to the archbishop for help. He took 50 soldiers with him and went to the bridge at midnight. As the carriage approached, the archbishop held up a **crucifix** and demanded the driver identify himself. But the carriage rushed past, and the archbishop and soldiers were thrown aside.

The archbishop gathered the townspeople. They dug up the governor's body and found it full of blood. His cheeks and lips were also red. The archbishop ordered a stake to be driven through the heart. Witnesses said as soon as the stake pierced the heart, the corpse groaned and a "jet of blood spurted high in the air."[7] Thanks to the archbishop, the vampire never troubled his bride again.

The Case of Mercy Brown

Doctors as well as priests were often consulted if vampire activity was suspected. One such doctor was Harold Metcalf, who tried to help the Brown family of Exeter, Rhode Island, in the 1800s. George and Mary Brown had six children, including daughters named Olive and Mercy, and Edwin, their only son. After Mary and Olive died, Edwin became sick. A short time later, Mercy also grew ill, and she died on January 17, 1892. She was nineteen years old.

Suspecting that a vampire might be to blame for the deaths, George Brown's neighbors told him he must dig up the bodies of his wife and daughters to see if they were decomposing properly. Reluctantly, he agreed and asked Metcalf for help.

On March 17, Metcalf examined the bodies of Mary, Olive, and Mercy Brown. He concluded that Mary and Olive were not vampires because their bodies had begun to decay. Mercy's body, however, looked alive. Witnesses also swore that her position in the coffin had changed since her burial.

Metcalf removed Mercy's heart and liver. Blood dripped from the heart, and the liver looked healthy, so the doctor told Mercy's father to burn the organs on a nearby rock. Then the father mixed the ashes with some medicine the doctor gave him. Metcalf told Edwin to drink the mixture to save himself. Edwin did as he was told, but it did not work. He died a few weeks later.

The Case of Toma Petre

Not all vampire slayings took place in the distant past. In fact, several men believe they exorcised a vampire in southwest Romania in 2004. The vampire's name was Toma Petre. He was a laborer who lived in the Romanian village of Marotinu de Sus. In December 2003, he had an accident while working in a field, and he died. Three months later, Petre's sister told some men in the village that Petre was making her daughter-in-law sick.

Buried Alive

Very sick people sometimes slip into a deep sleep called a coma. Years ago, some patients in comas may have accidentally been buried alive because their families believed they were dead. If the patients woke up, they struggled to escape. Being buried alive might explain why Mercy Brown's position in the coffin changed.

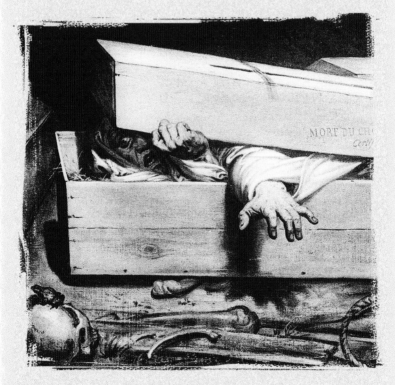

A man in a coma wakes in terror to find that he has been buried alive in a vault.

In this old illustration, a man drives a burning stake through a vampire's skeleton to make sure the beast will never rise again.

The men knew exactly what to do. First, they went to Petre's grave at midnight and dug up his body. Then, according to the *London Observer:* "They split his rib cage with a pitchfork, removed his heart, put stakes through the rest of his body and sprinkled it with garlic. They burnt the heart, put embers in water and shared the grim cocktail with the sick woman."[8]

Soon, the daughter-in-law recovered, and the men were regarded as heroes. Like the men of Marotinu de Sus, vampire slayers were admired for their courage and their skill. Both hunting and slaying vampires were considered important and dangerous work.

Chapter 4

VAMPIRE HUNTERS

From centuries past to today, there have been people who search for vampires. They do this in a variety of ways. Many of them collect and investigate stories of vampire encounters and exorcisms to try to determine whether vampires really exist.

The Vampire Shepherd

Augustin Calmet, a French monk, was such an investigator. He studied eyewitness reports of vampire sightings and attacks in Czechoslovakia, Hungary, and Serbia. In 1746, he collected these reports in a book called *The Phantom World*. The book became very popular. In it, Calmet described a belief in "dead persons which suck the blood of the living."

He added, "This opinion has been confirmed by several facts of which I believe there can be no doubt, given the quality of the witnesses."[9]

One case that Calmet recorded involved a shepherd who had lived four hundred years before in

French monk Augustin Calmet described several vampire sightings in his book, *The Phantom World.*

the village of Blow in western Czechoslovakia. After he died, he began appearing to people and calling them by name. Exactly eight days after seeing the shepherd, each person died.

The peasants became convinced the shepherd was a vampire. So they dug up his body and tried to stake it to the ground. But the shepherd laughed at them and said he would use the stake to scare away dogs.

That night, the shepherd choked several villagers to death. The

DISSERTATIONS
SUR LES
APPARITIONS
DES ESPRITS,
ET SUR LES
VAMPIRES
OU LES REVENANS DE
Hongrie, de Moravie, &c.
Par le R. P. Dom AUGUSTIN CALMET,
Abbé de Senones.
Nouvelle Edition revuë & corrigée.
PREMIERE PARTIE.

A EINSIDLEN
Dans la Princiere Abbaïe par Jean Everhard Kälin,
M.DCC.XLIX.
Avec Approbation & Privilége.

Originally written in French, The Phantom World included the story of a Czechoslovakian vampire shepherd.

next morning, the peasants loaded his body onto a cart so it could be taken out of town to be burned. On the way, "the corpse howled like a madman and moved his hands and feet as if alive,"[10] wrote Calmet. The villagers decided to pierce the shepherd's body again and again with stakes until all the blood poured out. Only then did they determine the vampire shepherd was really dead.

The Vampire of Serbia

Another case Calmet investigated was that of Arnald Paul, a vampire who stalked the Serbian village of Madreiga. Paul died after being crushed to death by a falling cart. Thirty days after his death, four of his neighbors suddenly and mysteriously died as well.

The villagers remembered a story Paul had told them about being attacked by a vampire when he was a soldier in Greece. He said he had cured himself by eating dirt from the grave of the vampire who had bitten him. Quickly, the villagers dug up Paul's body and found it to be suspicious. The skin had a healthy-looking red complexion, and the nails and beard were longer. Worst of all, "fresh blood . . . flowed from his eyes, nose, mouth, and ears,"[11] wrote an eyewitness. In fact, Paul's **shroud** was soaked with blood.

To destroy the vampire, a village official drove a stake through Paul's heart. When he did, the body "**emitted** a piercing scream, as if still alive,"[12] wrote Calmet. So the official cut Paul's head off and burned his body. Immediately the mysterious deaths stopped.

The Highgate Cemetery Vampire

Although Calmet investigated vampires long ago, vampire hunters are still at work today. Sean Manchester, for example, believes he has found and destroyed many vampires over the last 35 years. Manchester's most famous case is that of the Highgate Cemetery Vampire.

Highgate Cemetery is located in London, England. In the late 1960s, several people reported seeing a tall, dark figure walking through the cemetery at night. They said when this figure looked at them, they felt as if they were being hypnotized. One witness, David Farrant, said the figure was over 7 feet (2.13m) tall and had eyes that "were not human."[13] At the same time, police were finding dead dogs and foxes in the cemetery with their throats cut and their bodies drained of blood.

Then a sixteen-year-old girl named Elizabeth Wojdyla reported that she and a friend had seen dead bodies leave their graves and roam about. Shortly

In the late 1960s, teenager Elizabeth Wojdyla reported seeing corpses rising from the graves at London's Highgate Cemetery.

thereafter, Elizabeth started to have nightmares. Her head hurt, she lost weight, and she felt sick to her stomach. When her boyfriend found two puncture wounds on her neck, he decided to call Manchester.

Inside the Crypt

Manchester told Elizabeth she had been attacked by a vampire. In October 1970, he decided to perform an exorcism to help Elizabeth get better. One afternoon, he went to the crypt where he suspected the vampire was entombed. He and three assistants carried a stake, garlic, salt, holy water, incense, candles, and crosses.

Inside the crypt, he found a mysterious-looking coffin that was missing a nameplate. Carefully he lifted the lid. "There it lay," recalled Manchester. "A body which appeared neither dead nor alive."[14] Suddenly the air grew cold, and the candles flickered.

Manchester knew the sun was setting and that the vampire could awaken at any moment. He quickly sprinkled the body with garlic, salt, and holy water. Then he commanded the evil spirit to leave the body. Nothing happened. Instead, "the [vampire's] glazed eyes stared horribly, almost mocking me,"[15] he wrote later. He fled the vault before darkness fell to avoid a vampire attack.

Manchester returned to conduct another exorcism one year later, but the vampire was gone. A **psychic** told Manchester the vampire had moved to another location. Two years later, people reported seeing and hearing strange things in an abandoned mansion in north London, not far from Highgate Cemetery. Manchester wondered if the house was the new **lair** of the Highgate Cemetery vampire.

He and two assistants decided to investigate during the daytime. As they entered the house, fog surrounded them. The air was cold, and they smelled a terrible odor.

Manchester explored the basement and found a coffin. He and his assistants carried the coffin outside behind the mansion and opened it. Inside they saw the same vampire as before.

Manchester did not hesitate. He grabbed his stake and hammer. "With a mighty blow," he wrote, "I drove a stake through the creature's heart, then shielded my ears . . . [from] a terrible roar."[16] Seconds later, the vampire's body turned to smelly brown slime. Manchester and his assistants poured gasoline on top of the casket and lit a match. As they watched the casket burn, Manchester hoped the Highgate Cemetery vampire would never bother anyone again.

The Royal Street Vampire

Like Manchester, Kalila Katherina Smith, founder of the New Orleans **Paranormal** and **Occult** Research Society, is another modern-day vampire hunter. She claims to have been attacked by a vampire in a series of dreams. The vampire attacks started in the early 1990s while Smith was investigating a house on Royal Street in New Orleans. The house belonged to an 18th-century chemist named Jacques St. Germaine, who dabbled in the occult. St. Germaine liked to lure young women to his home so he could bite their necks and drain their blood, which he kept in wine bottles.

Soon after Smith began investigating St. Germaine's house, she began to have strange dreams. In these dreams, Smith writes, she was bitten by a "wolf-like creature."[17] Another time, she felt something heavy press down on her while she lay sleeping: "I could not scream or move . . . I woke with a feeling of numbness in my left shoulder blade."[18] Later, she developed a mysterious 3-inch (7.6cm) scar in the same shoulder blade.

Then one day while she was walking past the house, Smith had a vision of the vampire that had been attacking her. He was a "tall, gaunt man with

Actor Jude Law plays a hungry vampire in the 1998 film *The Wisdom of Crocodiles*. Vampires have been the villains of countless horror movies.

Casket Girls

Legend says vampires were smuggled into New Orleans in 1728 by young women who were called casket girls because they traveled with coffin-shaped boxes. When the city's death rate doubled a year later, people blamed the increase on vampires. More than likely, though, the city's many criminals were behind the deaths.

wolflike eyes that glowed red," she recalled. "His hands were long and thin with **elongated** claws. He was pale and drawn."[19] The vision lasted only a few seconds. The vampire attacks stopped shortly thereafter.

Smith is not the only person, past or present, to believe in vampires. But most doctors, scientists, and historians agree that the creatures do not really exist. Nevertheless, stories of vampire sightings and attacks are entertaining ones that can make an audience shudder and scream!

Notes

Chapter 2: Vampire Sightings and Attacks

1. Quoted in Rosemary Ellen Guiley, *Vampires, Werewolves and Other Monsters*. New York: Visionary Living, 2005, p. 279.
2. Quoted in Michael E. Bell, *Food for the Dead*. New York: Carroll and Graf, 2001, p. 66.
3. Quoted in Guiley, *Vampires, Werewolves and Other Monsters*, p. 87.
4. Quoted in Rosemary Ellen Guiley, *The Complete Vampire Companion*. New York: Macmillan, 1994, p. 184.
5. Quoted in Guiley, *The Complete Vampire Companion*, p. 184.

Chapter 3: Vampire Slayers

6. Quoted in David J. Skal, ed., *Vampires: Encounters with the Undead*. New York: Black Dog and Leventhal, 2001, p. 25.
7. Quoted in Skal, *Vampires*, p. 30.
8. *London Observer*, "A Village Still in Thrall to Dracula," June 20, 2005, p. 6.

Chapter 4: Vampire Hunters

9. Quoted in Marie-Helene Huet, "Deadly Fears: Dom Augustin Calmet's Vampires and the Rule

over Death," *Eighteenth Century Life*, May 1997, p. 227.

10. Quoted in Skal, *Vampires*, p. 24.
11. Quoted in Paul Barber, "The Real Vampire," *Natural History*, October 1990.
12. Quoted in Huet, "Deadly Fears," p. 227.
13. Quoted in Bill Ellis, "The Highgate Cemetery Vampire Hunt: The Anglo-American Connection in Satanic Cult Lore," *Folklore*, 1993, p. 21.
14. Quoted in Skal, *Vampires*, p. 531.
15. Quoted in Skal, *Vampires*, p. 531.
16. Quoted in Skal, *Vampires*, p. 533.
17. Kalila Katherina Smith, *Journey into Darkness: Ghosts and Vampires of New Orleans*. New Orleans: DeSimeon, 2004, p. 153.
18. Smith, *Journey into Darkness*, p. 154.
19. Smith, *Journey into Darkness*, p. 154.

Glossary

crucifix: A Christian symbol of Jesus dying on a cross.

decompose: To rot away.

elongated: Lengthened or extended.

emitted: Sent out.

exhumed: To be taken out of the earth.

exorcise: To drive away evil spirits.

hypnotized: To put into a state of sleep.

lair: A bed or resting place of a wild animal.

legends: Popular stories, sometimes believed to be true.

occult: Involvement with the supernatural.

omen: A thing that predicts something good or bad.

paranormal: Pertaining to the spirit world.

psychic: A person who is said to be able to communicate with the spirit world.

shroud: A burial cloth.

superstitious: Having a belief based on fear or ignorance rather than scientific fact.

For Further Exploration

Books and Articles

Daniel Cohen, *Real Vampires*. New York: Scholastic, 1996. A fascinating collection of vampire stories and vampire folklore from around the world.

Martin Jenkins, *Informania: Vampires*. Cambridge, MA: Candlewick, 1998. After opening with a comic-book version of Dracula, this entertaining book offers stories of vampire investigations, descriptions, and photographs of bloodsucking animals; a history of vampire folklore; a list of vampire movies; and a "Vampire Hunter's Survival Guide."

Raymond Miller, *Vampires*. San Diego: KidHaven, 2004. This book explores vampire myths and folklore as well as Hollywood's portrayal of vampires in the movies.

Weekly Reader Senior, "Vampire's Vacation," November 8, 2002. A fun and interesting article about Dracula Land, a Transylvanian theme park that shows visitors how a real-life prince named Vlad the Impaler became the inspiration for Bram Stoker's novel *Dracula*.

Web Sites

Vampire Bats (www.nationalgeographic.com/kids).

Contrary to vampire folklore, vampire bats do not attack humans. This site offers fun facts about vampire bats and how they really find and drink the blood they need to survive.

Vampires: Fact or Fiction (www.library.thinkquest.org/5482) Why is Transylvania so important to vampire lore? How does one kill a vampire? What are vampire bats? Find the answers to these questions and more by visiting this site.

Index

About the Author

Bonnie McMeans is an English professor and free-lance writer who enjoys writing for children. She has a bachelor's degree in social anthropology and a master's degree in journalism. Recent publications include "Tales from the Tomb" for *Hopscotch* magazine and a biography of filmmaker James Cameron. She is married, has three children, and lives in Havertown, Pennsylvania.